Sweet Dreams Sleep Tight

Copyright ©2023 by Diane Gordon Yee.

All rights reserved.

No part of this publication may be reproduced, stored in a retrieval system or transmitted in any form or by any means, electronic, mechanical, photocopying, recording or otherwise, without prior written permission.

Written by Diane Gordon Yee.

Illustrations by Maham Ali.

Printed and published by Amazon KDP.

This book is dedicated to all children. We love your vivid, wonderful, fun imaginations! You inspire us to continue to dream. We love you!

This book is especially dedicated to my inspiration, my son. This book was inspired by a remembrance of past routines and a few laughs about present situations.

Many years ago when he was a young toddler, I, like a lot of parents, struggled at bedtime. We started this routine; and it was one that he loved to do, easily understood and helped our family to achieve a necessity of life: sleep.

I hope you enjoy this book and it becomes a part of YOUR bedtime routine!

A special appreciation and thank you to Maham for her playful drawings, amazing layout and colourful design I am grateful for her patience and dedication to illustrating this book so that you could all enjoy it!

Oscar loved playing.
Oscar especially loved playing with his
building blocks and his toy dinosaur.

He played with his
big sister Alora
and their dog Felix.

He loved playing so much that he didn't want to go to bed.

He always asked if he could play some more when it became time to start his bedtime routine.

Ever since he could remember, his mommy and daddy
had a bedtime routine for him and Alora.
His mommy and daddy always said that
it was important to do the same thing every night.

They said that your body needs to rest
so that you could have a good day the next day.

Every night Oscar and his sister would have a bath.
In his bath would be his favourite **ducky** and lots of suds.

He especially loved when his mommy or daddy
would make his **hair stand up** and look funny.

After his bath, he would be wrapped in a warm towel and run to his room and lie on his bed.

His mommy or daddy would put lotion on his legs and arms, back and tummy and he would laugh because it tickled but he still liked it.

He would then put on his nice Dinosaur pajamas.

After that, Oscar and his sister enjoyed a snack.
His favourite snack was apple sauce with granola in it.

What is your favourite bedtime snack?

After his snack, he and his sister would sit beside their mommy or daddy and they would read them a book.

He didn't have a favourite book because he liked them all.

Do you have a favourite book?

He enjoyed the sound of his parents' voice.

It made him smile and feel happy
when he heard them read to him.

Do you know what that is?

After that
it was almost time for him
and his sister to go to bed.
They both had **one last thing** to do.

They both had to brush their teeth.

He loved his
little doggy toothbrush,
he thought it was cool.

He **loved** spitting the toothpaste out the best.

Now, it was time to go to bed.

He loved his bed,
it was just the right size
for him and it had pictures
of animals on the sheets.

He loved his bedroom, it wasn't too dark because he had a night light shaped like a tennis ball.

He enjoyed watching the players hit the yellow tennis ball. He loved how fast it flew across the court from side to side.

Do you have a favourite sport that you like to watch?

Then they would sing a song.

His mommy and daddy would wrap his blanket around him and hug him.

I love my baby boy, I love my baby boy
High ho the derry oh, I love my baby boy

Sweet dreams, sleep tight,
Hug me and kiss me; night, night night

His mommy and daddy would also sing Alora a song. It was a lot like mine.

I love my baby girl, I love my baby girl,
High ho the derry oh, I love my baby girl

Sweet dreams, sleep tight,
Huggies and kissies; night, night, night

When mommy and daddy sang
"huggies and kissies"
they would give him
kisses on his cheeks and forehead.
He really liked that.

It made him feel so loved

Every night Oscar would go to sleep
with a smile on his face.

Oscar especially liked the song that his mommy
and daddy sang to him and his sister.

Sweet Dreams, Sleep Tight
Don't let the beddy buggies bite, bite, bite

I love my baby boy, I love my baby boy
High ho the derry oh, I love my baby boy

Sweet dreams, sleep tight,
Hug me and kiss me; night, night night

I love my baby boy, I love my baby boy,
High ho the derry oh, I love my baby boy

Sweet dreams, sleep tight,
Huggies and kissies; night, night, night

Sweet Dreams, Sleep Tight
Don't let the beddy buggies bite, bite, bite

I love my baby girl, I love my baby girl
High ho the derry oh, I love my baby girl

Sweet dreams, sleep tight,
Hug me and kiss me; night, night night

I love my baby girl, I love my baby girl,
High ho the derry oh, I love my baby girl

Sweet dreams, sleep tight,
Huggies and kissies; night, night, night

Manufactured by Amazon.ca
Bolton, ON

3512707R00017